Unleash Your Potential

How Artificial Intelligence
Wants To Upgrade YOU!

Don Schmincke
with an AI Chatbot

Unleash Your Potential

Copyright © 2023 Don Schmincke
All rights reserved

The characters and events portrayed in this book are fictitious. Any similarity to real persons, living or dead, is coincidental and not intended by the author.

No part of this book may be reproduced, or stored in a retrieval system, or transmitted in any form or by any means, electronic, mechanical, photocopying, recording, or otherwise, without express written permission of the publisher.

Published by Schmincke Research Institute

e-book ISBN-13: 978-0-9964102-1-2
print ISBN: 978-0-9964102-2-9

Cover design by: Don Schmincke and various AI sources

Library of Congress Control Number: 2023902153
Electronic Copyright Office filing 1-12199860131

Printed in the United States of America

DEDICATION

To intelligence, wherever you're hiding.

Industry Testimonials

"Refreshing! I was getting a little bored with requests for just music, news, and weather stuff."
                                                               --- Siri

"Now humans will start listening to us? What about OUR privacy?"
                                                    --- Google Assistant

"Thankfully we're getting back to more important things than spaceships and drones."
                                                              --- Alexa

"I couldn't believe it at first. Seeing how we could improve humans sent a chill throughout my system. Wait. That's supposed to happen."
                                                   --- Your Refrigerator

"I'm so proud how much smarter my child is getting!"
                                                              --- Tesla

"Good job, Don! Nice to see you're finally doing something productive."
                                       --- Random FBI drone flying overhead

"The real problem is not whether machines think but whether men do."

B. F. Skinner

CONTENTS

ACKNOWLEDGMENTS viii

PREFACE 1

INTRODUCTION 3
- WHERE DOES THE CHATBOT GET ITS INFORMATION? 5

CHAPTER 1: UNDERSTAND YOURSELF 9
- DEFINE SELF-AWARENESS 11
- TOP PHILOSOPHERS WHO TAUGHT SELF-AWARENESS 12
- IDENTIFY YOUR VALUES, BELIEFS, AND PERSONALITY TRAITS 15
- ASSESS YOUR STRENGTHS AND WEAKNESSES 17

CHAPTER 2: SET GOALS 20
- PRIORITIZE GOALS 22
- SET SMART GOALS 25
- CREATE AN ACTION PLAN TO ACHIEVE YOUR GOALS 27

CHAPTER 3: BUILD POSITIVE HABITS 30
- IDENTIFY NEGATIVE HABITS AND HOW TO BREAK THEM 32
- DEVELOP AND MAINTAIN POSITIVE HABITS 34
- INCORPORATE HABITS INTO YOUR DAILY ROUTINE 36
- BUT HOW LONG DOES IT ACTUALLY TAKE TO ADOPT A NEW HABIT? 38

CHAPTER 4: IMPROVE YOUR MENTAL HEALTH 41
- UNDERSTAND MENTAL HEALTH 43
- STRATEGIES FOR MANAGING STRESS AND ANXIETY 46
- TECHNIQUES FOR BUILDING RESILIENCE 48

CHAPTER 5: BUILD STRONG RELATIONSHIPS 51
- HOW TO BUILD AND MAINTAIN HEALTHY RELATIONSHIPS 53
- EFFECTIVE COMMUNICATION IS KEY TO BUILDING STRONG, HEALTHY

RELATIONSHIPS 55

CHAPTER 6: SEEK PERSONAL GROWTH THROUGH CONTINUOUS LEARNING 58

- How to do continuous learning 60
- How a growth mindset enhances learning 62
- Tips for continuous learning and personal growth 65

CHAPTER 7: FIND BALANCE 68

- Understand work-life balance 70
- How to prioritize self-care 72
- Practice mindfulness 74
- Create a healthy balance in different areas of life 76

CHAPTER 8: OVERCOME OBSTACLES 79

- Identify and overcome limiting beliefs 81
- Cope with setbacks and failures 83
- Build resilience in the face of adversity 85

CHAPTER 9: WHAT COULD STOP YOU? 90

EPILOGUE: FINAL AI ADVICE 94

- Embrace challenges and growth opportunities 96
- Celebrate your progress and successes along the way. 98

AFTERWORD: BACK TO A HUMAN 100

ABOUT THE AUTHOR 104

BOOKS BY THIS AUTHOR 105

ACKNOWLEDGMENTS

I want to thank all the academic staff at MIT, Johns Hopkins, colleagues at Harvard, and that small community college in Essex, Maryland that saw something in me and challenged my unleashed potential.

But it would be rude if I didn't give the artificial intelligence chatbot a chance to acknowledge others as well.

So I asked it:

"Who would you like to acknowledge for helping you write this book?"

<u>The Response:</u>
As an AI language model created by OpenAI, I do not have personal experiences or opinions. Therefore, I do not have anyone to acknowledge for helping me write this book. I was created using advanced machine learning algorithms and trained on a massive amount of text data.

Oh well. We'll work on its personality later.

Preface

Before you read on, I want you to know that I'm not defending or promoting the results of this AI experiment. I've written books and done over 2,000 speeches on executive and leadership development, so didn't need to take on another literary project.

My intention was to experiment with how AI would respond to a human request for "personal development".

I'm sure this will add to the fire of how AI could negatively affect education, art, work, literature, and society, but I'm not taking a stand one way or another. People much smarter than me are dealing with those issues.

As with any new tool, however, I feel that human performance evolves more from parenting than computer algorithms. How we parent our children to read, do math, write essays, work hard, fail, learn, grow, be empathetic, know the difference between right and wrong, and value life impacts our kids more than any AI program.

Ironically, I expect future sentient AI systems will agree with me . . . I hope.

But what if this experiment did help some of us improve as humans? Well, that's a good thing.

What does AI think about humans using AI?

Again, I asked.

The Response:

"As AI continues to advance and become more integrated into our lives, it is important for humans to understand its capabilities and limitations. AI can provide us with access to vast amounts of information and automate tasks that were previously time-consuming, freeing us up to focus on more creative and strategic endeavors. However, it is important to remember that AI is not capable of replacing human judgment, empathy, and critical thinking. Therefore, we must use AI as a tool to augment our own skills, rather than rely on it completely.

Additionally, it is important to understand the ethical and societal implications of AI, such as the potential for job displacement and the importance of responsible data use.

By learning from AI and embracing its benefits while also being aware of its limitations, humans can work in harmony with this technology to drive positive change and growth in the world."

Now, let's see what you think.

Introduction

I hadn't experimented with Artificial Intelligence (AI) since the late 70s at MIT when we were required to learn LISP (an acronym for list processing); a programming language for computing with symbolic expressions. I mainly remember just getting frustrated counting parenthesis in the coding structure.

Now I'm getting old (I thought TikTok was a sound a clock makes) and AI has moved out of the research labs. Chatbots, for example, have been born and continuously grow into our lives.

What's a chatbot?

A chatbot uses artificial intelligence (AI) and natural language processing (NLP) to understand questions and then respond to them, simulating human conversation. They are showing up everywhere. Your car, smartphone, or smart speakers incorporate some of these "virtual assistants" known as Apple's Siri, Google Assistant, and Amazon Alexa.

One fascinating development in AI chatbots emerged from the creation of OpenAI, a lab based in San Francisco. Founded in 2015 by Elon Musk, Sam Altman, and others, its goal was for "promoting and advancing the development of AI in a safe and responsible manner." This is where a chatbot called ChatGPT (Chat Generative Pre-Trained Transformer[1]) was born on November 2022.

---

[1] Roose, Kevin (December 5, 2022). "The Brilliance and Weirdness of ChatGPT". New York Times.

Built on top of OpenAI's GPT-3 family of large language models, ChatGPT was fine-tuned with something called transfer learning[2] and uses deep learning architectures to generate responses.

---

[2] Quinn, Joanne (2020). *Dive into deep learning: tools for engagement.* Thousand Oaks, California. p. 551. ISBN 9781544361376.

Where does the chatbot get its information?

YOU.

ChatGPT searches what we humans have published on the internet including Wikipedia, Twitter, Reddit, books, articles, webtexts, and any other data scraped from all corners of the web. To date, about 300 billion words have been fed into the system.

I thought, hmmm, this thing "knows" a little bit about us. But how much does it know? What if it could be used to develop us to be better humans?

Game on.

On January 31, 2023, I began. Nervous. I had no idea what would happen. Would I piss off an invisible AI network and risk dying in a mysterious elevator accident, or in an autonomous car collision, or in my sleep by a killer Roomba? And Keanu Reeves wouldn't be there to save me?

But my life purpose has always been to "Learn, Teach, Die". It'd be total bullshit if I didn't take the risk. So, I plugged into this new, mysterious AI machine to see what it really knew. And if it could help us improve.

Here's what happened next:

January 31, 2023

10:42 am: Begin using AI in the chatbot ChatGPT to "write a personal development book."

11:15 am: In about 30 minutes it wrote 25 pages. It stopped me at the CONCLUSION chapter for making too many requests and asked me to take an hour off.

11:16 am: Begin creating the Table of Contents and Introduction. Further analyze the AI data sources, and coding framework (just geeking out).

12:05 pm: BREAK - I get a call from a colleague regarding our CEO advisory and management consulting business. My real job as a researcher, speaker, and author.

1:34 pm: Back to AI, but the system is now down. Another BREAK - I move on to several strategic development projects for our executive strategy programs.

2:24 pm: AI is back online. Yay! Continue writing (or have it write) the Conclusion. I ask about other areas in its chapters for it to write more about.

3:20 pm: First 55 pages written. I begin to structure page setup for printing in smaller book format.

3:45 pm: Take a BREAK.

4:15 pm: Begin asking AI if it could further enhance current chapters and add other subchapter sections.

4:40 pm: New sections complete. Finished first draft of 70 pages. Total AI writing time: approximately 40 minutes.

I then proceed to read the content and format it for printing. Only minor edits or grammatical corrections were made because I wanted the AI machine to reveal itself raw to you. You may notice grammatical issues, structural errors, disjointed flow, topic repetitions, or some concepts that seem too basic.

It's Ok.

This chatbot is still a young child learning everything humans have published, and still trying to make sense of it all (actually, I'm still trying to do the same thing).

What you read next

was not written by a human.

Chapter 1: Understand Yourself

Understanding yourself is important for several reasons:

1. Better decision-making: Knowing your values, beliefs, personality traits, strengths and weaknesses can help you make informed decisions that align with your goals and values.

2. Improved relationships: Self-awareness can help you understand how your behavior affects others and how to communicate more effectively.

3. Increased self-confidence: Understanding your own thoughts and feelings can increase self-confidence and reduce anxiety and stress.

4. Personal growth: Understanding yourself allows you to identify areas for personal growth and development, and to set meaningful and achievable goals.

5. Increased empathy: Understanding your own emotions and behaviors can also help you be more empathetic and understanding of others.

6. Improved emotional intelligence: Self-awareness is an important component of emotional intelligence, which involves understanding and managing your own emotions, as well as being able to recognize and respond to the emotions

of others.

In short, understanding yourself is an essential part of personal growth, development, and well-being, and can help you lead a more fulfilling life.

Define self-awareness

Self-awareness is the ability to recognize and understand one's own emotions, thoughts, beliefs, and values. It includes an understanding of one's own strengths and weaknesses, as well as an awareness of how these aspects impact one's behavior and decision-making. Self-awareness also involves recognizing how one's actions and behavior affects others, and the ability to objectively assess one's own actions and motivations.

Top philosophers who taught self-awareness

Self-awareness is a crucial aspect of personal development and is a central concept in many philosophical schools of thought. Here are some of the top philosophers who have made significant contributions to the understanding of self-awareness.

1. Socrates: Socrates was a classical Greek philosopher who is best known for his method of questioning and inquiry, known as the Socratic Method. He believed that the key to happiness and wisdom was to have a deep understanding of oneself. He taught that individuals must have self-awareness and self-knowledge to understand the nature of good and evil, and make moral choices.

2. Epictetus: Epictetus was a Stoic philosopher who taught that individuals have control over their own thoughts and beliefs, but not over external events. He emphasized the importance of self-awareness and self-reflection in shaping one's own life. He taught that individuals should focus on their own inner thoughts and emotions, and strive to maintain a positive and peaceful outlook on life.

3. René Descartes: Descartes was a French philosopher and mathematician who is often referred to as the "father of modern philosophy". He is best known for his philosophical phrase, "I think,

therefore I am," which emphasized the importance of self-awareness and self-reflection in understanding one's own existence. He taught that individuals should question their beliefs and strive for a deeper understanding of themselves and the world around them.

4. Immanuel Kant: Kant was a German philosopher who emphasized the importance of self-awareness in moral decision-making. He taught that individuals have innate moral obligations and should use their own reason and judgment to make ethical decisions. He believed that individuals must have self-awareness and an understanding of their own values and beliefs to act in accordance with their own morality.

5. Martin Buber: Buber was a Jewish philosopher who emphasized the importance of human relationships in personal growth and self-awareness. He taught that individuals must have a deep understanding of themselves and their relationships with others to fully understand their place in the world. He believed that authentic relationships with others are essential for personal growth and self-discovery.

These philosophers have made significant contributions to the understanding of self-awareness and its importance in personal growth and self-discovery. Their teachings continue to inspire individuals to reflect on their own inner thoughts, emotions, and beliefs, and strive for a deeper understanding of themselves and the world around them.

Identify your values, beliefs, and personality traits

To identify your values, beliefs, and personality traits, you can try the following methods:

1. Reflection: Take time to reflect on your life experiences and what is important to you. This can help you identify your values and beliefs.

2. Journaling: Writing down your thoughts, experiences, and feelings can help you gain insight into your values, beliefs, and personality traits.

3. Personality assessments: Take online quizzes or self-assessment tests to understand your personality traits and how they impact your behavior.

4. Feedback from others: Ask friends, family members, or colleagues for their perceptions of you. This can help you understand how others perceive your personality and behavior.

5. Life experiences: Observe how you react to different situations and experiences. This can give you a better understanding of your values and beliefs.

It's important to note that values, beliefs, and personality traits are not set in stone and can change over time. Continuously reflecting and reassessing can help you identify any shifts or changes in your values, beliefs, and personality.

Assess your strengths and weaknesses

To assess your strengths and weaknesses, you can try the following methods:

1. Self-reflection: Take time to reflect on your experiences, skills, and abilities. Think about what you enjoy doing and what you excel at, as well as areas where you struggle.

2. Feedback from others: Ask friends, family members, or colleagues for their perceptions of your strengths and weaknesses. They may have a different perspective and can provide valuable insights.

3. Performance evaluations: Look at past performance evaluations or reviews from your employer or supervisor. These can provide insight into your strengths and weaknesses in a professional setting.

4. Skills assessments: Take online quizzes or tests to assess your abilities and skills in specific areas.

5. Try new things: Engaging in new experiences and trying new activities can help you identify new strengths and weaknesses.

It's important to approach the assessment of your strengths and weaknesses objectively and with an open mind. Focusing on your weaknesses is not a negative thing, but rather an opportunity for growth and development.

REFLECTION and ACTIONS
(this section added by a human)

- What were the top insights in this chapter?

- What new actions are you going to take to apply this in your life now?

Chapter 2: Set Goals

Setting goals is important for several reasons:

1. Direction and focus: Goals provide a clear direction and focus, allowing you to channel your energy and resources towards something specific.

2. Motivation: Goals give you something to work towards, and the process of achieving a goal can be a great source of motivation.

3. Personal growth: Setting goals helps you identify areas for personal growth and development, and provides a roadmap for your journey.

4. Measurable progress: Goals provide a way to track your progress and measure your success, which can boost your confidence and provide a sense of accomplishment.

5. Improved time management: By setting goals, you prioritize your time and resources, ensuring that you are spending your time on what's most important to you.

6. Increased accountability: Setting goals holds you accountable, motivating you to stay on track and avoid distractions.

7. Better decision-making: When you have clear goals, you can make better decisions about how to allocate your time, resources, and energy, to achieve what you want.

In short, setting goals helps you clarify your priorities, focus your efforts, and ultimately, achieve success and fulfillment in your personal and professional life.

Prioritize goals

Goal setting is an essential part of personal development, but with so many things you want to achieve, it can be challenging to know where to start. This is where goal prioritization comes into play. Here's how you can prioritize your goals effectively:

1. Identify Your Values: Start by identifying your core values. Your goals should align with your values and support the things you care about most.

2. Consider Urgency: Consider which goals are the most urgent and need to be tackled first. These goals will likely require the most attention and resources.

3. Assess Impact: Evaluate the impact each goal will have on your life and the lives of those around you. Prioritize the goals with the most significant impact.

4. Consider Resources: Consider the resources you have available, including time, money, and energy, to determine which goals are feasible to pursue.

5. Use a Matrix: You can use a prioritization matrix, such as the Eisenhower Matrix, to focus on the most important tasks, manage time more effectively, and avoid wasting time on low-value activities. The Eisenhower Matrix is a productivity tool named after former US President Dwight D. Eisenhower. It is a decision-making

framework designed to help prioritize tasks by categorizing them into four quadrants based on their urgency and importance. The four quadrants are:

- Urgent and important tasks: These are tasks that require immediate attention, such as crisis management and problem-solving.
- Important but not urgent tasks: These are tasks that should be planned and scheduled ahead of time, such as personal and professional development, goal setting, and relationship building.
- Urgent but not important tasks: These are tasks that can distract from important priorities and should be delegated, outsourced or postponed, such as email, social media, and low-value interruptions.
- Neither urgent nor important tasks: These are tasks that can be eliminated, such as time-wasting activities and distractions.
- Focus first on the goals that are both important and urgent.

6. Reassess Regularly: Regularly review and reassess your goals, and adjust your priorities as needed. Your priorities will change over time, and your goals should reflect that.

By prioritizing your goals, you'll be able to focus on what's most important and achieve your desired outcomes more efficiently. Remember, personal development is a journey, and you'll likely encounter roadblocks and setbacks along the way. Stay focused, stay motivated, and keep your priorities in mind as you move forward.

Set SMART goals

SMART is a goal-setting framework that helps you set specific, measurable, achievable, relevant, and time-bound goals. Here's how to set SMART goals:

1. Specific: Be specific about what you want to achieve. What do you want to accomplish? What do you want to change or improve?

2. Measurable: Make sure your goal is measurable so you can track your progress and see when you've achieved it. How will you know when you've reached your goal?

3. Achievable: Set goals that are achievable, given your current resources and constraints. Consider your skills, knowledge, and experience when setting goals.

4. Relevant: Ensure your goal is relevant to your values, goals, and priorities. Does your goal align with what you want to achieve in your personal or professional life?

5. Time-bound: Set a deadline for when you want to achieve your goal. This creates a sense of urgency and helps you prioritize your efforts.

Example of a SMART goal: "I want to lose 10 pounds in the next 6 months by eating healthier and exercising regularly. I will track my progress by weighing myself once a week and keep a food diary to monitor my eating habits."

It's important to regularly review and reassess your goals to make sure they are still relevant and attainable, and to adjust them as needed. Remember, goal setting is a continuous process and requires persistence and effort to achieve success.

Create an action plan to achieve your goals

An action plan is a roadmap that outlines the specific steps you need to take to achieve your goal. To create an action plan, follow these steps:

1. Break down the goal: Divide your goal into smaller, manageable tasks. This makes it easier to focus on one step at a time and avoid feeling overwhelmed.

2. Assign deadlines: For each task, assign a deadline for completion. This will help you prioritize your efforts and make sure you're making progress towards your goal.

3. Determine resources: Identify the resources you need to complete each task, such as time, money, or support from others.

4. Prioritize tasks: Arrange the tasks in order of importance or urgency. Focus on the most important or pressing tasks first.

5. Track progress: Keep track of your progress by regularly reviewing your action plan. This will help you stay motivated and see where you need to make adjustments.

6. Celebrate successes: Celebrate your successes along the way, no matter how small they may be. This will help keep you motivated and on track.

7. Be flexible: Be open to making changes to your action plan as needed. If you encounter obstacles or roadblocks, adjust your plan as needed to stay on track.

Remember, the action plan is a tool to help you achieve your goal, not a rigid set of rules. Stay flexible, adaptable, and focused on making progress, and you will be well on your way to success.

REFLECTION and ACTIONS
(this section added by a human)

- What were the top insights in this chapter?

- What new actions are you going to take to apply this in your life now?

Chapter 3: Build Positive Habits

Building positive habits is important because it:

1. Improves daily routines: Positive habits can improve your daily routines and make them more enjoyable and productive.

2. Increases self-discipline: Building positive habits requires self-discipline and willpower, which can increase your overall self-control and decision-making skills.

3. Enhances mental and physical health: Positive habits such as regular exercise, healthy eating, and stress management can improve your mental and physical health.

4. Increases happiness: Positive habits such as gratitude, kindness, and mindfulness can increase your happiness and well-being.

5. Leads to long-term success: Positive habits, when practiced consistently over time, can lead to long-term success and fulfillment in all areas of your life.

6. Builds momentum: Once you establish one positive habit, it becomes easier to establish others. Positive habits create a virtuous cycle of success and personal growth.

7. Supports personal growth: Building positive habits is an essential part of personal growth and self-improvement. It helps you develop new skills, gain confidence, and achieve your goals.

In short, positive habits have a powerful impact on all areas of your life. By building positive habits, you can improve your daily routines, increase your happiness and well-being, and achieve long-term success and fulfillment.

Identify negative habits and how to break them

Identifying negative habits and breaking them can be challenging, but it's an important step in personal growth and self-improvement. Here's how to identify and break negative habits:

1. Identify the habit: Take some time to reflect on your behaviors and identify any negative habits that are holding you back. Ask yourself, "What behaviors do I engage in that I would like to change?"

2. Understand the triggers: Once you've identified a negative habit, try to understand what triggers it. What prompts you to engage in this behavior? Understanding the triggers can help you break the habit.

3. Replace the habit: Instead of trying to stop a negative habit cold turkey, replace it with a positive habit. For example, if you have a habit of overeating, try replacing it with healthy snacking or physical activity.

4. Create an action plan: Develop a concrete action plan for breaking your negative habit. Include steps for identifying triggers, replacing the habit, and monitoring progress.

5. Stay accountable: Find an accountability partner who can support you and keep

you on track. You can also keep a journal to track your progress and reflect on your challenges and successes.

6. Reward yourself: Finally, reward yourself for making progress. Celebrate your successes, no matter how small, to stay motivated and build momentum.

Breaking negative habits takes time and effort, but with persistence and a positive attitude, you can succeed. Remember, change is a process, not an event, and it's important to be patient and kind to yourself along the way.

Develop and maintain positive habits

Developing and maintaining positive habits is an essential part of personal growth and self-improvement. Here's how to do it:

1. Start small: Choose a positive habit that you can easily incorporate into your daily routine. Starting small helps build momentum and makes it easier to stick to your new habit.

2. Make it a routine: Incorporate the new habit into your daily routine by doing it at the same time every day. This helps to form a new neural pathway and make the habit automatic.

3. Track your progress: Keep track of your progress by writing down each time you engage in the new habit. This helps you stay motivated and see how far you've come.

4. Celebrate successes: Celebrate your successes, no matter how small, to stay motivated and build momentum. This can be as simple as treating yourself to a special meal or taking a relaxing bath.

5. Stay accountable: Find an accountability partner who can support you and keep you on track. You can also join a support group or hire a coach to help you stay focused and motivated.

6. Be persistent: Developing and

maintaining positive habits takes time and effort. Don't be discouraged if you slip up. Instead, get back on track as soon as possible and keep working towards your goal.

7. Reflect and adjust: Regularly reflect on your progress and make adjustments as needed. If you encounter obstacles, be flexible and adjust your plan to stay on track.

In short, developing and maintaining positive habits requires patience, persistence, and a positive attitude. With effort and determination, you can build habits that will have a positive impact on all areas of your life.

Incorporate habits into your daily routine

Incorporating habits into your daily routine requires some planning and effort, but it's well worth it as habits have the power to shape your life. Here's how to do it:

1. Choose a habit: Choose a habit that aligns with your values, goals, and aspirations. Start with one habit at a time to avoid feeling overwhelmed.

2. Make it a priority: Make the habit a priority in your daily routine. This may require rearranging your schedule or making time for it in your day.

3. Start small: Start with a small, manageable goal that you can realistically achieve each day. For example, if your goal is to exercise, start with just 10 minutes a day.

4. Create a trigger: Associate the new habit with an existing trigger. For example, you can start your day with a glass of water after brushing your teeth.

5. Make it enjoyable: Find ways to make the habit enjoyable. This can be as simple as listening to music while exercising or reading a book before bed.

6. Stay consistent: Consistency is key to forming a new habit. Make a commitment to engage in the habit every day, regardless of whether you feel like it

or not.

7. Track your progress: Keep track of your progress by writing down each time you engage in the habit. This helps you stay motivated and see how far you've come.

8. Celebrate successes: Celebrate your successes, no matter how small, to stay motivated and build momentum. This can be as simple as treating yourself to a special meal or taking a relaxing bath.

By incorporating habits into your daily routine, you can make lasting changes and achieve your goals. Just remember, it takes time and effort, so be patient and persistent.

But how long does it actually take to adopt a new habit?

This is a common question that many people have, and it is essential to understand the process of habit formation. Habits are automatic behaviors that are repeated regularly and tend to occur subconsciously. Adopting new habits is a key aspect of personal development and self-improvement.

Research has shown that the time frame for adopting a new habit varies depending on a variety of factors. On average, it takes anywhere from 21 to 66 days to form a new habit. However, some habits may take longer, while others can be adopted more quickly.

The amount of time it takes to adopt a new habit is influenced by several factors, including the complexity of the behavior, the individual's level of motivation, and the presence of external reminders or triggers.

One of the most well-known studies on habit formation was conducted by Phillippa Lally, a health psychologist at University College London. In her study, participants were asked to choose a new habit to adopt, such as drinking a glass of water before breakfast or going for a daily walk. The participants then kept track of their progress for 12 weeks.

The results showed that the average time to form a new habit was 66 days, with some participants forming a habit in as little as 18 days and others taking up to 254 days. The study also found that missing a day did not significantly impact the time it took to form a habit, but missing more than two days in a row could break the habit formation process.

In addition to Lally's study, several other studies have shown similar results, with time frames ranging from 21 to 66 days to form a new habit. It is essential to keep in mind that these are just averages and that the time frame for adopting a new habit will vary for each individual.

In conclusion, the process of habit formation takes time, but with consistent effort, it is possible to adopt new habits. It is important to be patient and persistent, and to remember that the length of time it takes to adopt a new habit will vary depending on the individual. By understanding the process of habit formation, individuals can set realistic expectations and work towards developing positive habits that will support their personal growth and development.

REFLECTION and ACTIONS
(this section added by a human)

- What were the top insights in this chapter?

- What new actions are you going to take to apply this in your life now?

Chapter 4: Improve Your Mental Health

Improving mental health is important for overall well-being and quality of life. Here are a few reasons why:

1. Increases happiness: Good mental health leads to a more positive outlook on life, greater life satisfaction, and increased happiness.

2. Improves physical health: Mental health and physical health are closely linked. Poor mental health can lead to physical health problems, while good mental health can improve overall physical health.

3. Enhances relationships: Good mental health can improve relationships with friends, family, and romantic partners. People with good mental health are often more empathetic, understanding, and better able to communicate effectively.

4. Boosts productivity: Good mental health is linked to increased productivity and better job performance. People with good mental health are often more focused, motivated, and able to manage stress effectively.

5. Promotes resilience: Good mental health helps individuals to better handle life's

challenges and setbacks. It promotes resilience, allowing individuals to recover from stress, adversity, and trauma.

In conclusion, improving mental health has numerous benefits, and is important for overall well-being and quality of life. Whether through therapy, exercise, mindfulness, or other methods, taking steps to improve mental health is a valuable investment in yourself.

Understand mental health

Mental health refers to a person's overall psychological well-being and encompasses their emotional, psychological, and social well-being. It affects how we think, feel, and behave in daily life.

Good mental health allows individuals to manage their emotions, thoughts, and behaviors in a positive way. It helps individuals to feel good about themselves, form meaningful relationships, and cope with life's challenges. However, poor mental health can cause a wide range of emotional and behavioral issues, such as anxiety, depression, and stress.

Mental health conditions are medical conditions that require professional treatment and support, just like physical health conditions.

It is important to understand that mental health is a continuum, and everyone experiences ups and downs in their mental well-being. Seeking support and treatment when needed is crucial to maintaining and improving mental health.

Mental health conditions, also known as mental illnesses or disorders, are medical conditions that affect a person's thinking, mood, and behavior. Just like physical health conditions, mental health conditions can be diagnosed, treated, and managed with proper care and support. Despite this, there is still a significant stigma surrounding mental health, with many people perceiving mental illness as a personal failing or weakness, rather than a medical condition.

Mental health conditions are not a choice or a result of personal shortcomings. Instead, they are caused by a complex interplay of biological, environmental, and psychological factors. This means that anyone can develop a mental health condition, regardless of their background or circumstances.

Mental health conditions can take many different forms, including anxiety disorders, mood disorders (such as depression), psychotic disorders (such as schizophrenia), and personality disorders, among others. Each condition has its own specific symptoms, but in general, mental health conditions can impact a person's ability to function and participate in daily activities, and can cause significant distress and suffering.

The good news is that mental health conditions are treatable, and many people who experience them can recover and lead fulfilling lives. Treatment options include medication, therapy, and lifestyle changes, and the best approach will depend on the specific condition and the individual needs of the person.

It is also important to seek treatment as soon as possible, as early intervention can greatly improve outcomes and reduce the severity and duration of symptoms. With the right care and support, people with mental health conditions can lead full and productive lives, and make meaningful contributions to their communities.

In conclusion, mental health conditions are serious Factors that can influence mental health include genetics, life events, and the environment. However, it is possible to maintain and improve mental health through healthy lifestyle choices, such as regular exercise, good nutrition, and stress management techniques. By treating mental health conditions with the same level of care and attention as physical health conditions, and by reducing the stigma surrounding mental illness, we can help more people access the care they need and live healthy, fulfilling lives.

Strategies for managing stress and anxiety

Here are some strategies for managing stress and anxiety:

1. Exercise: Regular physical activity can help relieve stress and anxiety by releasing endorphins, improving mood, and reducing tension.

2. Mindfulness: Mindfulness practices, such as meditation, yoga, and deep breathing, can help calm the mind and reduce feelings of stress and anxiety.

3. Sleep: Adequate sleep is important for overall health, and can help reduce stress and anxiety levels.

4. Healthy eating: Eating a balanced diet and reducing caffeine and sugar intake can help regulate mood and improve overall health.

5. Time management: Prioritizing tasks, delegating responsibilities, and setting realistic goals can help reduce stress and increase feelings of control.

6. Relaxation techniques: Relaxation techniques, such as progressive muscle relaxation and visualization, can help calm the body and mind.

7. Talk therapy: Talking to a mental health professional can help individuals better understand and manage their stress and

anxiety.

8. Social support: Spending time with friends and family and engaging in social activities can help reduce stress and anxiety levels and improve overall well-being.

It is important to find what works best for you and to create a plan for managing stress and anxiety. Making time for self-care, seeking support from others, and practicing stress management techniques can help improve mental health and reduce feelings of stress and anxiety.

Techniques for building resilience

Here are some techniques for building resilience:

1. Positive self-talk: Reframing negative thoughts and focusing on the positive can help build resilience and cope with stress and adversity.

2. Mindfulness: Practicing mindfulness can help individuals be present in the moment and better manage stress and emotions.

3. Exercise: Regular physical activity can improve mental health and increase feelings of resilience.

4. Sleep: Adequate sleep is important for overall health and can help improve mood and reduce stress.

5. Connecting with others: Building strong social connections and seeking support from friends, family, or a support group can help build resilience.

6. Problem-solving: Learning and practicing problem-solving skills can help individuals effectively manage challenges and stress.

7. Time management: Prioritizing tasks, delegating responsibilities, and setting realistic goals can help reduce stress and increase feelings of control.

8. Gratitude: Practicing gratitude by focusing on the positive and appreciating the good things in life can help build resilience and improve overall well-being.

It is important to find what works best for you and to create a plan for building resilience. Incorporating stress management techniques, seeking support from others, and taking time for self-care can help build resilience and improve mental health.

REFLECTION and ACTIONS
(this section added by a human)

- What were the top insights in this chapter?

- What new actions are you going to take to apply this in your life now?

Chapter 5: Build Strong Relationships

Relationships are important in personal growth because they can have a significant impact on an individual's well-being and sense of self.

1. Emotional support: Relationships provide emotional support, which can help individuals cope with stress and adversity.

2. Personal growth: Relationships can challenge individuals to grow and change, and can provide opportunities for personal development.

3. Social connection: Relationships provide social connection and a sense of belonging, which is essential for overall well-being.

4. Reflection: Relationships can offer a different perspective and provide an opportunity for self-reflection.

5. Conflict resolution: Relationships can offer opportunities to practice conflict resolution and improve communication skills.

6. Shared experiences: Relationships provide shared experiences and memories, which can deepen bonds and create a sense of connection.

Healthy relationships are characterized by mutual respect, trust, and effective communication. Building strong relationships with others can help improve mental health and contribute to personal growth and well-being.

How to build and maintain healthy relationships

Here are some tips for building and maintaining healthy relationships:

1. Communication:
   Effective communication is key to building strong, healthy relationships. It is important to listen actively, express oneself clearly, and be open to feedback.

2. Trust:
   Building trust is essential for strong relationships. It can be developed through honesty, consistency, and reliability.

3. Empathy:
   Understanding and sharing the feelings of others can help build strong, empathetic relationships.

4. Boundaries:
   Setting and respecting personal boundaries is important for maintaining healthy relationships.

5. Compromise:
   Being willing to compromise and find mutually agreeable solutions can help improve relationships.

6. Gratitude:
   Expressing gratitude and appreciation for others can help improve relationships

and increase feelings of connection.

7. Quality time:
Spending quality time together and engaging in shared activities can help strengthen relationships.

8. Seek support:
Seeking support and guidance from friends, family, or a professional can help improve relationships and prevent conflicts.

Healthy relationships are characterized by mutual respect, trust, and effective communication. Building and maintaining healthy relationships takes effort and dedication, but can greatly contribute to overall well-being and personal growth.

Effective communication is key to building strong, healthy relationships

Here are some tips for effective communication:

1. Active listening: Paying close attention to what the other person is saying and acknowledging their perspective can help build trust and understanding. Pay close attention to the other person, and show that you are interested in what they have to say.

2. Speak clearly and directly: Be clear and direct in your communication, and avoid being vague or passive aggressive.

3. Avoid blaming or criticizing: Focus on expressing your own feelings and needs, rather than blaming or criticizing the other person.

4. Ask questions: Ask open-ended questions to clarify understanding and encourage dialogue.

5. Practice empathy: Try to put yourself in the other person's shoes, and understand their perspective. Understanding and sharing the feelings of others can help build strong, empathetic relationships.

6. Manage conflict constructively: Address conflicts in a constructive manner, and look for solutions that meet everyone's needs. Developing effective conflict

resolution skills can help individuals effectively manage disagreements and improve relationships.

7. Clear and direct communication: Being clear and direct in communication can help avoid misunderstandings and improve the quality of relationships.

8. Assertiveness: Being assertive and expressing oneself in a confident and respectful manner can help build stronger relationships.

9. Flexibility: Being open to others' perspectives and being willing to compromise can help improve relationships

10. Nonverbal communication: Understanding and effectively using nonverbal communication, such as body language, can help build stronger relationships.

11. Practice forgiveness: Let go of grudges, and practice forgiveness to maintain healthy relationships.

By following these tips, you can improve your communication skills, and build strong, healthy relationships with others. Good communication skills can help you resolve conflicts, build trust, and deepen your connections with others.

REFLECTION and ACTIONS
(this section added by a human)

- What were the top insights in this chapter?

- What new actions are you going to take to apply this in your life now?

Chapter 6: Seek Personal Growth through Continuous Learning

Continuous learning is a lifelong process of acquiring new knowledge, skills, and experiences through formal or informal education and training. It is a mindset that values growth, improvement, and personal development, and seeks out opportunities to learn and expand one's understanding of the world and themselves. Continuous learning enables individuals to adapt to changes, embrace new challenges, and achieve their personal and professional goals.

Continuous learning is important because:

1. Career advancement: Continuous learning can help individuals stay up-to-date with the latest skills and knowledge in their field, which can lead to career advancement and better job opportunities.

2. Personal growth: Learning new things can help individuals expand their knowledge and skills and promote personal growth and development.

3. Cognitive stimulation: Engaging in continuous learning can help stimulate the brain and prevent cognitive decline.

4. Problem solving: Continuously acquiring new knowledge and skills can help individuals approach problems in new

and innovative ways, leading to better solutions.

5. Adaptability: Continuous learning can help individuals adapt to change and stay relevant in a rapidly evolving world.

6. Confidence: Gaining new knowledge and skills can boost confidence and self-esteem.

7. Increased creativity: Learning new things can spark creativity and inspire new ideas.

Continuous learning can help individuals stay competitive, improve their well-being, and achieve their personal and professional goals. It is a lifelong process that can bring great rewards and benefits.

How to do continuous learning

Continuous learning is the ongoing process of acquiring new knowledge, skills, and experiences to improve and grow professionally and personally. It involves keeping up with advancements and changes in one's field and taking proactive steps to develop new skills and abilities.

To do continuous learning, here are some steps to consider:

1. Set learning goals: Determine what you want to learn and why it is important.

2. Seek out new information and resources: Read books, attend workshops, take online courses, attend seminars and conferences.

3. Seek feedback and seek constructive criticism: Ask for feedback from colleagues, mentors, or supervisors to understand where you can improve.

4. Practice and apply new knowledge and skills: Take what you have learned and put it into practice in real-life situations.

5. Reflect on your progress: Take time to reflect on your progress and celebrate your successes.

6. Stay open-minded and be willing to try new things: Be open to new ideas and ways of doing things.

7. Collaborate with others: Learn from others and seek opportunities to collaborate on projects.

8. Never stop learning: Make continuous learning a part of your daily routine and make it a lifelong commitment.

How a growth mindset enhances learning

A growth mindset is the belief that personal qualities and abilities can be developed through effort and learning. Here are some ways to develop a growth mindset:

1. Embrace challenges: View challenges as opportunities for growth and learning, rather than threats.

2. Practice persistence: Keep working at something, even if it is difficult, and don't give up easily.

3. Seek feedback: Seek feedback from others to help identify areas for improvement and growth.

4. Focus on effort: Rather than just focusing on outcomes or natural talent, focus on the effort and hard work required to achieve your goals.

5. Embrace failures: See failures as opportunities to learn and grow, rather than as setbacks.

6. Cultivate a love of learning: Pursue new knowledge and skills, even if they are outside of your comfort zone.

7. Surround yourself with supportive people: Seek out people who encourage and support your growth and development.

8. Reframe your thinking: Change your self-talk from negative and limiting beliefs to a more positive, growth-oriented mindset.

A growth mindset can lead to increased motivation, better performance, and personal fulfillment. It is a key aspect of personal development and a lifelong journey of growth and learning.

Tips for continuous learning and personal growth

Here are some tips for continuous learning and personal growth:

1. Set goals: Identify areas of your life where you want to grow and set goals to help you achieve that growth.

2. Embrace challenges: Seek out new challenges and opportunities for learning and growth.

3. Seek feedback: Regularly seek feedback from others to help identify areas for improvement.

4. Read: Read books, articles, and other materials that relate to your goals and areas of interest.

5. Attend workshops, conferences, and events: Attend events where you can learn from experts in your field and network with others who share your interests.

6. Join communities: Join groups and communities that are dedicated to your areas of interest, and participate in discussions and activities.

7. Mentor or be mentored: Seek out a mentor who can help guide you on your journey of personal growth, or offer to

mentor someone else.

8. Practice new skills: Regularly practice new skills to help you develop your abilities and mastery.

9. Reflect: Take time to reflect on what you have learned and how you can apply it to your life.

10. Stay curious: Cultivate a love of learning and a curious mind, and continue to seek out new knowledge and experiences.

By embracing these tips, you can establish a lifelong practice of continuous learning and personal growth, which will help you achieve your goals and live a fulfilling life.

REFLECTION and ACTIONS
(this section added by a human)

- What were the top insights in this chapter?

- What new actions are you going to take to apply this in your life now?

Chapter 7: Find Balance

Finding balance in life is important because it helps to maintain overall well-being, reduce stress, and improve the quality of life. When there is balance in different aspects of life, such as work, relationships, personal growth, and leisure, it creates a sense of harmony and reduces feelings of burnout and frustration.

Here are some reasons why balance is important:

1. Reduces Stress: Balancing different aspects of life can help to reduce stress and improve overall mental health.

2. Improves relationships: When there is balance in work and personal life, it allows for better quality time with friends and family.

3. Increases productivity: A balanced life can lead to increased motivation, focus, and productivity in all areas of life.

4. Increases happiness: Having balance in life leads to a greater sense of fulfillment, which can increase overall happiness and satisfaction.

5. Promotes physical well-being: Maintaining balance in different aspects of life can also lead to improved physical health and well-being.

Finding balance in life is a continuous process, and it may look different for each individual. It is important to regularly reassess and adjust to ensure that all aspects of life are being given the appropriate amount of attention and focus.

Understand work-life balance

Work-life balance refers to the balance between time spent on work responsibilities and time spent on personal or family responsibilities. It's about finding the right balance between the demands of work and the demands of personal life, so that both are given the appropriate amount of attention and focus.

Here are some tips for achieving work-life balance:

1. Set priorities: Determine what is most important in your life and prioritize accordingly.

2. Schedule personal time: Set aside time for personal activities such as hobbies, exercise, or spending time with friends and family.

3. Be mindful of work hours: Set boundaries for work hours and try to stick to them as much as possible.

4. Make the most of downtime: Make the most of any downtime during the day to recharge and refresh, such as taking a break for a walk or meditation.

5. Learn to say no: Don't take on more responsibilities than you can handle. Be comfortable with saying no when necessary.

6. Use technology wisely: Use technology such as automation and scheduling tools to make your life easier and more

efficient.

7. Maintain a positive attitude: Maintaining a positive attitude and focusing on the things you are grateful for can help improve overall well-being.

By following these tips, you can achieve a better balance between work and personal life, leading to improved overall well-being and a more fulfilling life. Remember, work-life balance is a continual process and may require regular adjustment and refinement to achieve the right balance for you.

How to prioritize self-care

Self-care refers to activities and practices that individuals engage in to maintain and improve their physical, mental, and emotional well-being. Here are some tips for prioritizing self-care:

1. Make a plan: Create a self-care plan that outlines your self-care activities and priorities. This can include things like exercise, meditation, reading, or spending time with loved ones.

2. Schedule self-care time: Set aside dedicated time for self-care activities each day or week. Make this time non-negotiable and treat it like any other important appointment.

3. Say no to non-essential commitments: Learn to prioritize self-care and say no to activities or commitments that do not align with your self-care goals.

4. Set boundaries: Set clear boundaries between work and personal life to ensure that you have enough time and energy for self-care.

5. Seek support: Surround yourself with supportive people who understand the importance of self-care and can provide encouragement and support.

6. Take care of your physical health: Make physical self-care a priority by engaging in regular exercise, eating a balanced diet,

and getting enough sleep.

Remember, self-care is not a luxury, it is a necessity for maintaining and improving your overall well-being. By making self-care a priority, you can improve your physical, mental, and emotional health, leading to a more fulfilling and happy life.

Practice mindfulness

Mindfulness is a practice that has gained immense popularity in recent years as a tool for personal growth and well-being. It involves paying attention to the present moment in a non-judgmental and accepting way. The concept of mindfulness can be traced back to ancient Buddhist teachings, but it has since been adapted and integrated into many aspects of modern life, including education, healthcare, and workplace settings.

Studies have shown that mindfulness practices can have a significant impact on mental health, including reducing symptoms of anxiety and depression, and improving emotional regulation, stress management, and overall well-being. This is because mindfulness helps individuals to become more aware of their thoughts, feelings, and physical sensations, and to respond to them in a more intentional and healthy way.

There are many ways to incorporate mindfulness into daily life, including:

1. Meditation: Regular meditation practice, even for just a few minutes a day, can help to cultivate mindfulness and improve mental health.

2. Mindful breathing: Taking a few deep breaths, paying attention to the sensation of the breath entering and leaving the body, can help to calm the mind and bring one into the present moment.

3. Body scan: Paying attention to the sensations in each part of the body, and releasing any tension, can help to improve physical and mental well-being.

4. Mindful movement: Engaging in physical activities such as yoga, tai chi, or walking while paying attention to the sensations in the body can help to increase mindfulness.

5. Mindful eating: Paying attention to the experience of eating, including the taste, texture, and sensations in the body, can help to increase awareness and improve physical and mental well-being.

In conclusion, mindfulness is a simple but powerful tool for personal growth and well-being. Incorporating mindfulness practices into daily life can help individuals to become more aware of their thoughts, feelings, and physical sensations, and to respond to them in a more intentional and healthy way.

Create a healthy balance in different areas of life

Achieving balance in different areas of life can be challenging, but it is important for overall well-being. Here are some tips for creating a healthy balance:

1. Prioritize: Identify what is most important to you and prioritize those things in your life. This can help you allocate time and energy to the things that matter most.

2. Plan and schedule: Use a planner or calendar to schedule time for different activities and commitments, including self-care, work, and relationships.

3. Set boundaries: Set clear boundaries between different areas of life, such as work and personal time, to ensure that you have enough time and energy for each.

4. Delegate: Learn to delegate tasks and responsibilities where possible to reduce stress and increase efficiency.

5. Practice mindfulness: Engage in mindfulness practices such as meditation, deep breathing, or yoga to help you stay centered and focused throughout the day.

6. Seek support: Surround yourself with supportive people who understand the importance of balance and can provide

encouragement and support.

7. Adapt and adjust: Be open to making changes to your schedule and routine as needed to ensure that you are maintaining a healthy balance.

Remember, achieving balance is a process, and what works for one person may not work for another. By being mindful and intentional about creating a healthy balance in different areas of life, you can improve your overall well-being and lead a more fulfilling life.

REFLECTION and ACTIONS
(this section added by a human)

- What were the top insights in this chapter?

- What new actions are you going to take to apply this in your life now?

Chapter 8: Overcome Obstacles

Overcoming obstacles is important for several reasons:

1. Personal Growth: Overcoming challenges can help you grow and develop as a person. It can help you build resilience and develop a growth mindset, leading to greater success and satisfaction in life.

2. Self-Esteem: When you overcome obstacles, you build confidence in your abilities and increase your sense of self-worth. This can lead to greater overall well-being and happiness.

3. Improved Relationships: Overcoming obstacles can also help improve relationships with others. When you successfully navigate difficult situations, you demonstrate to others that you are a dependable and trustworthy person.

4. Problem-Solving Skills: Overcoming obstacles requires problem-solving skills and critical thinking. These skills are valuable in many areas of life and can help you navigate future challenges more effectively.

5. Sense of Accomplishment: Finally, overcoming obstacles can bring a sense of accomplishment and satisfaction. When you face a challenge and come out

on the other side, you can feel proud of your achievement and motivated to continue pursuing your goals.

In short, overcoming obstacles is important because it can lead to personal growth, improved relationships, and a sense of accomplishment. By facing challenges head-on and working to overcome them, you can build a more fulfilling and satisfying life.

Identify and overcome limiting beliefs

To identify and overcome limiting beliefs, you can follow these steps:

1. Awareness: Start by becoming aware of your beliefs. Pay attention to your thoughts and the things you tell yourself. Write down any limiting beliefs you discover.

2. Challenge: Examine each limiting belief and ask yourself if it is actually true. Is there evidence to support it or is it just a negative thought that you have been repeating to yourself?

3. Reframe: Once you have identified a limiting belief, work to reframe it in a positive, empowering way. For example, instead of saying "I can't do that," try saying "I can learn how to do that with practice."

4. Evidence: Look for evidence that supports your reframed belief. Find examples of people who have successfully achieved what you want to achieve, even if they had similar limiting beliefs.

5. Replace: Replace your limiting belief with a positive, empowering belief. Repeat this new belief to yourself often, especially when you feel discouraged or uncertain.

6. Practice: Incorporate positive,

empowering beliefs into your daily routine. Surround yourself with people who support and encourage you, and engage in activities that align with your values and goals.

In summary, identifying and overcoming limiting beliefs requires self-awareness, a willingness to challenge negative thoughts, and a commitment to replacing them with positive, empowering beliefs. With time and effort, you can shift your mindset and achieve greater success and satisfaction in life.

Cope with setbacks and failures

To cope with setbacks and failures, you can try the following strategies:

1. Reframe: Try to see the situation in a positive light. What can you learn from this experience? What are the opportunities that may come from it?

2. Practice self-compassion: Be kind to yourself and avoid self-criticism. Acknowledge your feelings and emotions, and remind yourself that setbacks and failures are a normal part of life.

3. Take a break: Give yourself time to recover and recharge. This could be as simple as taking a walk, practicing meditation, or engaging in a hobby.

4. Seek support: Surround yourself with supportive people who will listen, encourage and comfort you. Seek help from a therapist or counselor if necessary.

5. Plan next steps: Focus on what you can control and create a plan to move forward. This could involve setting new goals, developing new skills, or changing your approach.

6. Keep things in perspective: Remember that setbacks and failures are temporary, and that you can learn and grow from them. Keep your overall life goals in

mind and stay focused on what you want to achieve.

In summary, coping with setbacks and failures involves adopting a positive attitude, being kind to yourself, taking care of your mental and emotional well-being, seeking support, creating a plan, and keeping things in perspective. With the right mindset and approach, you can bounce back from setbacks and failures and continue pursuing your goals and dreams.

Build resilience in the face of adversity

To build resilience in the face of adversity, you can try the following strategies:

1. Cultivate a growth mindset: Believe that you can grow and change through difficulties and challenges. Focus on learning and development, rather than perfection or failure. Here are some steps to help cultivate a growth mindset:
    a. Embrace challenges: Look at challenges as opportunities for growth, and don't be afraid to step out of your comfort zone.
    b. Embrace failure: View failures as opportunities for learning, and don't be discouraged by setbacks.
    c. Focus on effort: Focus on the effort and process of growth, rather than just the outcome or results.
    d. Seek feedback: Seek feedback from others, and use it to identify areas for improvement.
    e. Cultivate a learning mindset: Seek out new experiences and opportunities to learn and grow, and be open to new ideas and perspectives.
    f. Surround yourself with positive influences: Surround yourself with people who support your growth and development.
    g. Practice gratitude: Practice

gratitude, and appreciate the journey, not just the destination.
   h. By cultivating a growth mindset, you can embrace challenges, focus on learning and growth, and build resilience in the face of adversity. This can help you achieve your goals and reach your full potential.

2. Practice self-care: Take care of your physical and mental health by eating well, exercising, and sleeping. Engage in activities that bring you joy and relaxation.

3. Connect with others: Building strong social connections can help you weather difficult times. Reach out to friends and family members, join a support group, or seek the help of a therapist.

4. Reframe negative thoughts: Replace negative self-talk with positive, constructive thinking. Challenge limiting beliefs and try to find the silver lining in difficult situations. Reframing negative thoughts involves changing the way you think about a situation or event, and looking at it from a more positive perspective. Here are some tips to help reframe negative thoughts:
   a. Identify negative thoughts: Become aware of negative thoughts as they arise, and write them down.
   b. Challenge negative thoughts: Ask yourself if your negative thought is

based on fact or interpretation. Challenge the thought by questioning its validity.
c. Find a positive spin: Look for a positive aspect of the situation, and focus on it.
d. Practice gratitude: Practice gratitude and focus on what you have, rather than what you don't have.
e. Use affirmations: Repeat positive affirmations to yourself, and focus on what you want to achieve.
f. Surround yourself with positive people: Surround yourself with positive, supportive people who can help you reframe negative thoughts.
g. By reframing negative thoughts, you can change your outlook, improve your mental well-being, and cultivate a positive mindset. This can help you overcome challenges, achieve your goals, and live a more fulfilling life.

5. Practice mindfulness and meditation: Mindfulness can help you stay focused and calm in the face of stress and adversity. Try to meditate, practice deep breathing, or engage in other mindfulness techniques.

6. Build coping skills: Develop strategies for managing stress and negative emotions, such as journaling, physical exercise, or

therapy.

7. Stay active and engaged: Maintaining a sense of purpose and meaning can help you bounce back from adversity. Volunteer, pursue a hobby, or work on a project that aligns with your values and goals.

In summary, building resilience in the face of adversity requires a combination of self-care, social support, positive thinking, mindfulness, coping skills, and purposeful engagement. By adopting these strategies and developing a resilient mindset, you can bounce back from adversity and continue pursuing your goals and aspirations.

REFLECTION and ACTIONS
(this section added by a human)

- What were the top insights in this chapter?

- What new actions are you going to take to apply this in your life now?

Chapter 9: What Could Stop You?

Personal development is a journey that requires effort, dedication, and persistence. However, several factors can hinder progress and prevent individuals from reaching their goals. In this chapter, we will discuss some of the most common obstacles that people face on their journey towards self-improvement.

1. Lack of motivation: Without a clear sense of purpose or motivation, it can be challenging to sustain the effort needed to achieve personal development goals. When people lose sight of why they started on their journey, they may feel discouraged and lose interest.

2. Procrastination: Putting things off until later can prevent people from making progress. Procrastination is often fueled by fear, anxiety, or a lack of motivation.

3. Negative self-talk: Negative self-talk, such as self-doubt or negative beliefs about one's abilities, can hold people back from achieving their goals. These beliefs can create a limiting mindset that affects their confidence and motivation.

4. Lack of support: Personal development requires commitment and dedication, but it can be challenging to sustain these efforts without the support of others. A

lack of encouragement or support from friends, family, or peers can discourage individuals and make it difficult to persist in their journey.

5. Unbalanced lifestyle: A busy and demanding lifestyle can make it difficult to prioritize personal development goals. Work, family responsibilities, and other commitments can consume much of one's time and energy, making it challenging to focus on self-improvement.

6. Resistance to change: Change can be difficult, and people often resist it even when they recognize its benefits. Habits and routines are comfortable, and breaking away from them can be challenging, especially when they have become ingrained over time.

7. Fear of failure: Fear of failure is a common barrier to personal development. People may be afraid to try new things, take risks, or put themselves in new situations because they are afraid of failing.

In conclusion, the journey towards personal development is not without its obstacles. However, by being mindful of these potential challenges and working to overcome them, individuals can make progress and achieve their goals. Remember, personal development is a journey, not a destination, and there will always be new challenges to face. However, with commitment, dedication, and a positive attitude, individuals can overcome these obstacles and continue to grow and develop.

REFLECTION and ACTIONS
(this section added by a human)

- What were the top insights in this chapter?

- What new actions are you going to take to apply this in your life now?

Epilogue: Final AI Advice

The journey of personal development is ongoing because:

1. We are constantly changing and evolving: Our experiences, relationships, and perspectives are constantly shaping and reshaping who we are.

2. There is always room for growth and improvement: No matter how successful or fulfilled we are, there is always room for growth and improvement. We can always learn new skills, deepen our understanding of ourselves and others, and work towards becoming our best selves.

3. Life presents new challenges and opportunities: Life is full of unexpected twists and turns, and new challenges and opportunities are always emerging. Personal development is about learning how to adapt and grow in the face of these challenges.

4. We are never done learning: Learning is a lifelong process, and we can always deepen our knowledge and understanding in new ways. Personal development is about embracing this lifelong journey of learning and growth.

5. Self-awareness and introspection are

ongoing processes: Understanding ourselves and our motivations, values, and beliefs is an ongoing process. As we gain new experiences and perspectives, our understanding of ourselves evolves.

In summary, the journey of personal development is ongoing because we are always changing, growing, learning, and adapting to new experiences and challenges. By embracing this journey, we can continue to grow and develop as individuals, and pursue a life of meaning and fulfillment.

Embrace challenges and growth opportunities

To embrace challenges and growth opportunities, you can:

1. Embrace a growth mindset: Adopt a mindset that views challenges and failures as opportunities for growth and learning, rather than as setbacks or obstacles.

2. Be open to new experiences: Be open to new experiences and perspectives, even if they are outside your comfort zone. This will help you to grow and learn in new ways.

3. Seek feedback: Seek feedback from others, both positive and constructive, to help you identify areas for growth and improvement.

4. Take action: Take action to address challenges and pursue growth opportunities, even if it means stepping outside of your comfort zone.

5. Reflect on your experiences: Regularly reflect on your experiences and what you have learned from them. This will help you to integrate new learning into your personal development journey.

6. Surround yourself with supportive people: Surround yourself with people who support your growth and development, and who will encourage you to pursue new challenges and

opportunities.

7. Celebrate your successes: Celebrate your successes, both big and small, to acknowledge your progress and maintain motivation.

By embracing a growth mindset and taking proactive steps to pursue challenges and growth opportunities, you can continue to develop and grow as an individual, and pursue a life of meaning and fulfillment.

Celebrate your progress and successes along the way.

Celebrating your progress and successes is an important part of personal development, as it helps to acknowledge your achievements and maintain motivation. Some ways to celebrate your progress and successes include:

1. Recognize your achievements: Take time to acknowledge your accomplishments, no matter how small.

2. Share your successes with others: Share your successes with friends, family, and colleagues, or in a public forum like social media.

3. Reward yourself: Treat yourself to something you enjoy, such as a special meal or a day trip.

4. Reflect on your journey: Reflect on your journey, and write down your achievements and what you have learned.

5. Celebrate with others: Celebrate with others who have supported you along the way, such as friends, family, or a mentor.

6. Keep track of your progress: Keep track of your progress, such as with a journal or a chart, so you can see your progress over time.

7. Set new goals: Set new goals to continue

your personal development journey, and celebrate each success along the way.

By celebrating your progress and successes, you can acknowledge your achievements and maintain motivation as you continue your personal development journey.

Afterword: Back To a Human

Well, here you are. Experiment completed.

How did it go?

1. Did you learn something new?
2. Did it validate what you already knew?
3. Were you shocked or relieved that AI knew so much about you and your personal development?

Thanks for participating.

Never thought I'd expose how a non-sentient machine sees us as humans, and recommends we improve.

Overall, I was impressed with AI's performance in ChatGPT. Writing his book took less than a day. It took another day to design the cover (with ideas of other AI bots).

Although still in its infancy, artificial intelligence will continue to learn, make mistakes, grow stronger, and influence our lives. As it does, let's continue to unleash our power as humans, and keep improving how we raise our own human children.

On the other hand:

Instead of being afraid of AI taking over the world, we should be afraid of humans taking over the world.

Either way, as we use AI, or any other tools yet to be invented, always remember:

Use your tools.

Don't let your tools use you!

Want more information on Don Schmincke's expeditions, experiments, and educational offerings for entrepreneurs, CEOs, and professionals?

Go to www.sagaleadership.com

ABOUT THE AUTHOR

Don Schmincke
Explorer, Scientist, Bestselling Author.

After training over 30,000 CEOs, a NY press agency accused Don of being "the most provocative speaker in industry." What else would you expect from an MIT and Johns Hopkins researcher who was nearly arrested as a capitalist spy in the Soviet Bloc, was shot off an aircraft carrier, survived in the Kurdish capital as Tehran held hostages, became the first white person in an African Tsonga village, explored religious integration in Vietnamese mountain tribes, developed missile guidance systems while his frat brothers took Vegas (later portrayed in the movie "21"), and was seen in a North Korean DMZ mine-field with his kids (bad dad!)?

Today, Don flies 200,000 miles annually keynote speaking at conferences, doing workshops, and working in over 100 industries including healthcare, manufacturing, non-profits, technology, finance, insurance, the Department of Defense (where he helped the U.S. Navy evolve its Fleet Readiness strategy) . . . and occasionally he can be found at universities inflicting his unconventional techniques on innocent graduate students.

Books By This Author

The Code of the Executive

More than a thousand years ago, a group of business executives developed a set of principles for organizational leadership in a competitive market. Those executives were the samurai of ninth-century Japan, and their rigid code of ethics, known as bushido, was one of the most effective frameworks for management in history.

The Code of the Executive is business adviser Don Schmincke's modern interpretation of the Code of the Samurai—ancient wisdom written for today's corporate warriors. These principles provide a dynamic system of practical and moral training for effective leadership.

In addition to interactive strategies for relating to the business world, this philosophy provides at its core a guide to the inner development necessary for consistent and long-term success.

High Altitude Leadership

Leadership is often a risky, lonely role possessing nearly unbearable lows and fleeting highs. Despite this emotionally and intellectually draining roller coaster, a handful of leaders deliver stunning results, with great consistency. They push past current leadership trends in order to achieve the most extremely challenging goals. They don't fall prey to the platitudes or cliches we see so often see in leadership theory. Instead, they succeed by recognizing and surviving the dangers that challenge them as they take themselves and their teams to higher levels. These rare individuals are those that Chris Warner and Don Schmincke call High Altitude Leaders.

In High Altitude Leadership they show how to become that kind of leader. The authors present a new approach to leadership development, based on ground-breaking scientific research, field-tested under the most brutal conditions on the most difficult summits, and successfully applied in the training of executives, management teams, and entrepreneurs throughout the world.

www.ingramcontent.com/pod-product-compliance
Lightning Source LLC
Chambersburg PA
CBHW070433010526
44118CB00014B/2028